From an O.G. to GOD

Lisa Duffy-Finney

ISBN: 978-1-68524-785-0

Printed in the United States of America.

Disclaimer: For the cover, we do not own the rights to the Black and Mild image on the cover. It was used to enunciate the message of this book.

From O.G. To God

Table of Contents

Dedication

I dedicate this book to Shirley Duffy-Scott. I am so thankful to God. Only through Him have I made it this far. He is truly a forgiving God.

Also, to my daughter, your daughter, your son and you.

Jeremiah 29:11

For I know the plans I have for you," declares the Lord, "plans to prosper you and not to harm you, plans to give you hope and a future.

My Beginning to Highschool

I was born July 11, 1980, on the Eastern Shore of VA. From what I can remember, I always lived with my grandmother and her boyfriend, along with my brother, uncle and sometimes my mother when she was around, which wasn't a whole lot. My uncle's children lived with us also. My grandmom's house was a very loving home. She welcomed everyone. On the weekends, she would cook for everyone and at times, take in my cousins when they were having issues.

I was told Kenny was my father and a great father he was. But family members would say, "Kenny's not your daddy. Glen's your daddy."

That would make me so mad. My grandmom never spoke of this though. As a child, I looked to my dad as my hero, so it became very confusing hearing that he was not my real dad. It was like torture to me. My mother was always gone for long periods at a time, so my grandmom was mom to me.

Grandmom would work in the fields Monday through Friday. We didn't have much. By society's standard, we were considered poor. I remember not even having running water. We had to pump our water and use the bathroom in a bucket. Grandmom would prepare big meals almost every day, rolling out dumplings and she would make cakes and pies. I would be sitting at the table doing anything she asked, which wasn't much sometimes. I always made sure I brought in wood to keep the stove going. My grandma and her boyfriend, as I called "grandpop" would drink heavily on the weekends and would argue a lot.

I remember my mom would come and go. She was semi-involved in my life, when I was 5 or 6. When she would be around, I think my grandmother would try and make her be a mother, but my mom was still very young and she liked to dress up and go out. She loved the nightlife and attention. When she would go out, she would leave us with a guy named Zac that lived down the street. He was a so-called family friend and when she went out, he would babysit us. That's when my whole life changed. My grandmom and her boyfriend would have been drinking all day and asleep downstairs. My brother, three years younger than I was, would be asleep and Zac would begin to perform oral sex on me, and he did each time he would babysit us. I was just a little girl! I don't remember exactly what he said to me, but I never told anyone. This is my first time speaking of this, and I'm 40.

Eventually, we moved. Thank God, because he couldn't watch us anymore. Shortly after this, my mom was gone and I remember our grandmother taking us to see her at the county jail. She was gone for a while, which seemed like forever.

I remember her sending pictures home. I was in 3rd grade and I took the picture to school one day and showed my teacher because I loved my mom and I thought she was pretty.

Everyone knew everyone where I grew up. So the teacher asked me, "Where is your mom?" I lied and said, "Hawaii." And the whole class said, "No, she not." So the teacher said, "Where is she?" The whole class said, "In jail." I can't explain how I felt. From that day forward, everything was a blur.

I even failed 3rd Grade. I was embarrassed and felt lost.

The next year came, and I was back on track. I was an Honor Roll Student in the 4th Grade. My mom was out of jail by this time and things were looking up in my world. But, my mom only came back around for a short period of time. My father, Kenny, lived in Florida. I felt incomplete and began to harbor bitterness.

Sidenote: *Be mindful of decisions you are making around children or that concern them. They are paying attention and know more than you think they do.*

I will say that I went through a period as I grew older, where I didn't like my mom. Yes, I will always love her and still do. I was mad simply because she wasn't around. Being young, I didn't understand that she may have been going through some things herself. I just didn't understand why she kept leaving, especially when I needed her the most. I couldn't grasp why she did want to be around me, her little girl.

Some of the milestones include, when my period came on or telling me about the birds and bees. I just wanted to have mommy and daughter time. I would see her hang out with different ones and think to myself, "Why doesn't she want to hang out with me? The little girl in me just wanted her parents around, but God was my Mother and Father. Sometimes, I still cry, but God! Healing has come and continues to come through my tears.

As I went through my 5th-grade year, several things happened that would impact my young life, yet again. I remember I went to church with my cousin, Talita, and they had an altar call. She said, "Just tell the Pastor what you want prayer for." So I did and I said for my mom. I believe I remember him anointing me with oil as he prayed and the rest I can't explain, but I know now that was the Holy Spirit. During 5th grade and beyond, there was a group of mean girls that bullied me. They dressed well and had nice hairstyles. But they were so evil and I dealt with their taunts every day.

I remember one morning before school, my grandma's boyfriend came to my bedroom door and said, "Can I play with you?" I started jumping on the bed and said, "Yes." So he walked away and shut the door. It didn't dawn on me until a little later as to what he was really asking. This was not the only time this happened to me. I never told a soul and felt so confused. I am not even sure why I didn't tell my grandmom. I felt embarrassed and didn't know if they would be mad at me. Sidenote: Be very careful who are around your children. There were a lot of things that I suppressed through the years. As I recalled the incident and began to heal from molestation, I could only think, "Dude, you helped raise me and I called you pop pop." I knew my grandmom never knew this. I remember when I started my period, I didn't even tell her. I would grab toilet paper and put it in my underwear. I felt like I went into a secret closet to hide somewhere. I felt like I had to do everything on my own. I was hiding my shame. The sad part is that I was not even guilty of anything.

As I started the 6th Grade, I felt like this would start a new chapter in my life. I remember the first day was my worst day. I remember having a pair of sneakers called Chics. Again, we didn't have much and I was okay with it until that day. I was just happy to have new shoes. I remember sitting in the auditorium at school and some girls walked by and were laughing and talking about my shoes.

Then maybe a few weeks later, as I was getting off the bus, a girl who was in High School smacked me behind my head. It was so embarrassing. I was being picked on and made fun of and I didn't like it at all.

After that, I believed something just clicked in me. I wasn't the same anymore and I wasn't going to let anybody else hurt me anymore. I started to fight back. I wanted to fight with any and every one that even looked at me the wrong way. Around the same time, I started to feel some type of way about my mother. I told my grandmom about the situations that I experienced at school and she started hooking me up with name-brand shoes and started letting me pick out my own clothes. I was very tall and skinny, so I just dressed like a boy. I got into a lot of fights in Middle School and outside of school. I seemed to stand out. I found a new group of friends.

They were a few girls from a nearby town called Whitesville. We started hanging out all the time and most of us are still friends today.

Highschool to 25 Years Old

I began to rebel. I began to want to be over there a lot. I just wanted to hang out and have fun or smelling my piss, as my grandmom would say. I am fast-forwarding to High School. I think people wanted to try me because, at that point, I was fighting everywhere. I held on to the fact that nobody was going to hurt me anymore. I started to sneak out, smoke weed, not come home, be at hotel rooms with boys. I remember asking my grandma one day to go somewhere and she said no. I got smart with her and left out walking. Boy, I still regret that. She didn't deserve that. She was upset. She called my mother and said, "Come get her." So off to NJ, I went. I was basically still doing what I wanted. I felt some type of way towards her like, "You ain't never really been there for ME. Why you feel I have to listen to you!" That was short lived. A few weeks later, grandma came to pick me up. Thank you, Jesus.

I know that I had pain from my childhood that had to do with my mom and the molestation. I had a lot of anger built up inside of me. I just knew that I wasn't going to be pushed around. I had a point to prove, or so I thought. Two guys that I knew started calling me "O.G.," and the name spread like wildfire. I felt like I had to live up to it. I would fight anybody. It didn't matter if they were male or female. I would fight for my so-called friends, family or anyone I felt I needed to. Let's just say, a lot of battles that I fought weren't even mine.

Whitesville had a little club and I started to hang out more and more. Then, I started smoking weed and staying out all night. People didn't really like me but they respected me. So I'm back hanging out again at the club one night fighting as usual. Someone threw a whole can across the floor and hit me in my eye. My grandmother had to take me to the doctor. It was so bad. So by now, the whole school is calling me O.G.

I stopped going to school. Grandmom didn't know a lot of things I was doing, but she did put me on long-term birth control, before I started having sex. I have to say, "Thanks, grandma." Now looking back, she may have known but didn't argue with me too much. She would just always say, "I just want you to graduate, baby."

About four houses down from where we lived, there was a family and I was told that the children were my brother and sister. We started connecting the dots and began to hang out. We looked so much alike and there was no question that we were related. My brother was my age and we started hanging out and going to clubs. My sister was a little younger. I was drinking more heavily here. I had graduated from beer and wine to Hennessey.

When I was 18, I said, "Let me go find the man that they say is my father." They said my father lived in the same county as I did, and my other dad, the one who I knew as dad, lived in New Jersey. So I went and along with my brother, one of his other children, by a different woman, we found him. Mind you, we're the same age and only four months apart!

As we met him, Glen said, "Yeah, I knew you were my child, but your Mom said, this and that…." In my mind, I was thinking, "Dude, miss me with that crap. You knew you had a child in the same area and didn't fight to see me or even try to come to see me. My mom wasn't even around. You never came to my grandmom's house or asked to see me." He had a lot of poor excuses. It was hard for me to comprehend. My parents were no-shows in my life. I just wanted them to take notice of me. Later in my life, I had to free him and forgive him. Sidenote: I will say that today that my relationship with my biological father is not perfect, but we continue to work on it. I have to show him the love of Christ. I want to be a Godly example in his life.

As time went on, my dad, Kenny's mom, passed and that took me somewhere. She was an awesome grandmom! About a year later exactly, my grandmom, my life, and my only mom died of cancer! I felt like I was in whirlwind. They protected and truly loved me. I never hurt like that before and to be honest, it still feels fresh. They were my everything my world and the only one who really loved me was gone! I want to say after my grandmother passed, a while after, my mom came back to VA. and stayed. And some years down the line, she rededicated herself back to God.

I began to drink and I was drinking heavily, but before she passed, we went to sign me up for Job Corp. So when the time came, I went. My cousin was already there, but she didn't know I signed up. I buried how I felt and just survived there. I didn't have visitors. I spent Thanksgiving and Christmas there one year, so all this just made me harder. I ended up staying there. Two years came and went. I went to live with my older cousin, but I called her my aunt. She was loving. When I left Job Corps, I didn't have any money coming in at all. I began to have to steal to survive. I was stealing everything from food to panties. I ended up in jail a couple times. I was young, wild and free and really didn't care about nothing. I had jobs but didn't keep them long. I wanted to be in the streets. I tried selling crack, but that wasn't for me. As I stated, I started stealing whatever I could get my hands on. I went to jail a couple times for that.

Trying to get back on track, I ended up moving in with my other older cousin. She was more like my grandmom and that's what I needed. She eventually moved out and left the house with her daughter and me because we had jobs at Burger King. I started to fall back into drinking heavily again and not caring about myself. I was young, wild, free, loving and looking for love in all the wrong places. But, no matter where I found myself, I would always say this little prayer. "God, thank You for this day and night. Please let me see many more and please keep me from cancer and AIDS."

After a while, I ended up moving in with my mom, who was like living with a friend or sister. We never really established that mom and daughter relationship.

Sidenote: *My mom was not a bad person and was never mean. She was just young when she had me. I could've lived with her any time, but due to my bitterness and hurt I could not see this. I will say that when I got in my early or mid-20's, I really started to pray on our relationship because what girl doesn't want their mom in their life.*

There were no rules. I wouldn't have listened to her. I had more bad relationships than good relationships. I was back to doing me. I was going out every week drinking, smoking and just doing whatever I could get into. I do remember my mom had a VCR and had videos. Believe it or not, I learned a lot of life lessons watching Madea plays.

I remember being around 22 and my mom tried to get me to watch it and I said, "Mom, I'm not watching no Church play." But one day, I decided to watch a few and fell in love with the story lines. I ended up taking it to the hood and everyone loved, "Madea's Family Reunion." It wasn't only funny to me though, I was taking away the nuggets that were dropped.

> ***Sidenote:*** *Until this day, I love and enjoy the plays. My husband took me to the last play. It was my first time seeing it live, I was sooo happy.*

I left my mom's house and I started really living house to house, stealing, ended up going to jail and sleeping with older guys for money.

I remember during one time that I ended up in jail, three Christian ladies would visit me. They would take time to minister to me. They really taught me the Word. I appreciated their transparency and the fact that they showed the love of God to me despite what I was doing or where I was. What they told me did not fall on deaf ears, I just not ready to stop doing what I was doing. I made promises to God I didn't keep. When I got out of jail, I began doing the same crap all over again.

> ***Sidenote:*** *I still keep in touch with these ladies today. Good and positive relationship will help you grow. Keep them when you get them.*

I wasn't ready to fully submit to God. I started popping E pills. I wanted to try them. I never wanted to try cocaine or crack, because I saw how it effected family members and some of my closest friends. First, it was a pill here and there until I got connected with a guy who had unlimited access to them and they were plentiful. So my cousin, homeboy, Trip, and I would go on binges. The spirit of addiction began to take hold of me. I remember it was the week of my birthday. He literally gave me a whole sandwich bag full of E. pills. I remember being on an entire week-long binge. I was in the bathroom. I knew I didn't feel right and in my mind, I thought I could make it to the couch, but I passed out on the floor by the door. When I came to, my little cousin and a friend of mine were over top of me, pouring water in my face. The worst feeling in the world was looking at the hurt in my little cousin's eyes. That wasn't my last time popping pills, but eventually, I stopped.

In 2004, I went to live with Uncle Dione. I had a job, but was still doing things I should not have been doing. One night after I got off of work I told my homie, "Hold up, let me wash up. I want a roll to the club with you." After we went back and forth for a while, he said okay. As it was time to leave the club, his car wouldn't start. He said, "We have to find a ride home." We went our separate ways. I asked another homie I knew for a ride and he said, "Yes, no problem." Plus my friend, Shontave, was in the car with him.

When I got in the backseat, there was another girl in the car, one I've been fighting and I had beef with since I was 16. I got in anyway.

She was popping off at the mouth and I knew she wasn't talking to them. As we were pulling into my uncle's driveway, I just hit her. We ended up fighting. I got out of the car and ended up fighting more than one person, because her sister and cousin were following us. My friend didn't help. I was able to hold my own. I think my uncle came out of the house and the fight broke up.

He said, "Come, lay down, Lisa." I noticed my arm was bleeding, but didn't think anything of it. I said, "No, I'm gonna go down the street and drink a beer with Temus." As I was walking, I fell down on the side of the road in a ditch. I remember saying, "Hold up. I know I'm not drunk." Something was telling me that night not to drink any liquor at all and I didn't. Temus and Jeff ran down to me and they said, "O.G., don't hit us, but you're bleeding out of your chest." I said, "Aw, man!" I knew something was wrong.

They called the ambulance. When they got to the hospital, they said my lung was punctured. They brought a doctor in from Norfolk, VA. I spent 7 days in hospital. My mom and aunts would come. The look in my mom's eyes shifted me and I had to make a conscious choice to change.

After this happened, I was tired of everything! My friend came to visit that next morning and said, What we gonna do about this?" I said, "Nothing." In the past, I would've been ready to fight again. He was shocked because he knew how I rolled. I wasn't afraid by a long shot. I was just tired!

I needed a break from everything and everyone, so I called a friend I recently met a year before at a motorcycle street race and asked her if I could stay with her for two weeks. Two weeks turned into a few years. She would take good care of me, talk to me, tell me how pretty I was and that I could be doing much better with myself. But we all know the truth hurts, so we would fuss and cuss back and forth all the time. But she was right and no matter what people said about me or what I was still doing, she never judged me.

She never saw me without food or clothes. She loved me anyway, no matter what, and truly loved on me like the mom and sister I never had. As I lived with her, my next door neighbor would see me almost every day. He would say, "Lisa, you are going to be a housewife." This was when I was out there. I used to laugh and say that he was crazy.

I told you that I was all over the place. I ended up going to New Jersey with my mom, uncle, and one of my homegirls that I had met at a race. One day, I met a guy named Steve. He owned a barbershop and sold weed. He was not that cute, but he was very charming. To make a long story short, he came to visit me. He lived in New Jersey. I went to NJ so that we could see each other, and he got me an apartment in my hometown. So I thought I was important. We were taking trips. He was buying me bags, clothes, shoes and whatever I wanted.

We had a pound of smoke laying around just to smoke on and money to blow. He didn't live in VA, so I didn't have to deal with him every day. This was when my life took a turn for the worse.

It wasn't the first time. It was a repeating cycle of the worst all over again. There were just different scenarios.

25 Years and Beyond

My Relationship with God

So, now, it was 2005. I was 25 years old. I found out I was pregnant. I was hyped. It was my first time being pregnant. I told all of my family and friends but little did I know that Steve didn't want a baby. He began to say things to make me feel low. He would tell me, "I don't want no child by you." He said, "You're going to get an abortion." I was so afraid and I didn't know who to talk to. I went along with his wish. I had the abortion and it was the worst decision I ever made. I remember asking the lady to let me see the ultrasound and she said, "We don't do that because it may cause mental issues." But I went on and on and she let me see it. "It isn't moving," she said. From that point on, I was sick and tired of everyone and everything went through a rough patch. After it was done, I hated myself and him. I prayed and prayed. I would cry and pray, "God, please forgive me." I didn't forgive myself until 2018, as I was getting closer to the Lord. After this happened, we didn't last much longer!

I remember going to work one day shortly after having the abortion. I worked at Sonic. I wasn't in a good head space and I was hungry. I was too proud to ask for some food. I passed out at work and when I came to, there was a lady squatted down over me. I had never seen this lady at work before and didn't see her after she spoke to me. She said, "God has a calling on your life." To this day, I believe she was an angel.

As time went by, it was now 2009. I was getting tired of drinking, so I had tried to stop on my own. It worked for a little while, but then I was back at it. One day, I said, "I'm going to church today." My friend's mom said, "Sure. You can use the car to go." I got there an hour early, but I went back home. I think I only went one other time after that.

I began to think about the things my friend would say. So I picked up the phonebook and started calling different places to see if they were hiring. I ended up speaking with a lady. She said, "Can you come in today?" I said, "Sure, Ma'am!" My friend's son took me. She said, "Can you start tonight?" I replied, "Oh yes, Ma'am…." Things started turning around that day. See, God was with me even in the valley and I didn't even notice it yet. I worked there for four years.

Sometimes, I had to start walking there and walking back, but I was determined. During my 2nd or 3rd year there, I was talking to the Chef about finding a house. I was his prep person. A lady came through the backdoor and he said, "She own houses." So we began to talk and about a month later, I was moving into my OWN place, with no man. It was just Lisa and I did it on my own!

One day, my mom came back to my little trailer and she called me outside and said, "You know if the Lord gave it to you, He will take it away." I said, "What are you talking about?" She said, "You have to pay your tithes." I said, "Okay.

Do I pay out of my net or gross?" She told me what she was taught. But it didn't sit right, so I did my own research. I remember looking at YouTube on sermons on tithing! I found my answer. I really wasn't making much, but I paid tithes anyhow.

I even had an older guy I knew to come by my job to pick them up to carry to church. Then one day, he said, "Lisa, they want you to come down to the church." I said, "Who? Me? I'm not coming down there to be crying in front of all them people…." He just laughed and went on. (R.I.P. Red Boy).

I started dealing with a new guy. He said, "Lisa, come on, why you don't go to church?" My excuse was, "I didn't have a ride." Well, I didn't, but I got everywhere else I wanted to go and there was a church directly across the street from where I was living. As time went by, I realized that he was toxic. He was telling his baby's mom that I was a crackhead. She was calling my phone with the blah blah blah, but I wasn't responding.

One day in 2013, I was out and about, got a pill from someone I know. It had been a long while since I did and it didn't sit right, but I did it anyway. I had planned on hanging out, but I had to go home and lay down. I didn't feel good. I woke up vomiting everywhere. I felt like I was in such a depressed state. Even though on the surface, it looked like I had it all together, deep down, I was still hurt and broken because of all the things from my past. Most things, I didn't deal with. I pushed them to the side and hid them. I called my cousin, Tammy, and I think I said, "I'm just tired." She said, "What you wanna do?" I said, "I want to be saved." So she said, "Meet me up at the church, Tuesday night for Bible study." I said, okay. I went even though I was just a mess. I started going faithfully and I got myself a Bible.

I would read my Bible at night. I would only drink on Friday because I didn't want to feel bad on Saturday and I started asking God to take the taste from my mouth. He did, but I was still smoking weed and Black and Mild's. I ended up getting to clean the church and I was more than happy to do it. Plus, I could pray while I was there.

I was learning and beginning to know God and it felt good! Then, God told me to leave the guy alone, but y'all know how it is when we think we're in love. So I kept on dealing and he kept hurting me so deeply. I asked God to reveal it to me because sometimes we have to see it to believe it. And boom! It didn't take long and I ran into him and the girl at the Food Lion!

I started seeing an old homie, but he was definitely not the right one. Plus, he was still a playboy. Then, I started hanging out again, but that was short-lived. God had His hands on me. One night, I was getting ready to go to the club. I got in the shower and I started feeling bad. I ended up laying down and not going anywhere. God convicted me.

I went to church the next morning and told the congregation about it. I know it was God working in and through me. Through all this, I was still going to every Bible study and Sunday morning service and second service. I was committed to God and He was constantly working on me. God was showing me His hand. I got a better job, then a promotion, and a car.

I remember praying, "God, please send me the man You want me to have because whatever I'm doing ain't right." Plus, I had quite a few men before, so some would refer to someone like that as a whore. The truth was I just wanted to be loved. I was known as a gangster, so….God definitely had to orchestrate this for me.

I am moving forward to 2016. My relationship with the Lord was getting deeper. My friend hit me up one day and said, "O.G., can you go check on my dad?" I said, "Sure. No big deal!" So I went to his home to check on him and started to clean up around the house a little. He said, "My son-in-law is on his way." I said okay and carried on. The next day, I went back to help him out again and he said, "My son-in-law is on his way." I said, "Where is he? You said that yesterday" The "son in law" was married to his daughter back in 98 or so. The son-in-law finally got there. He was asking a friend of ours about me. He shut him down and said she can talk.

Interestingly enough, we began to talk. He lived in Baltimore, which was a 4-hour drive and had to be at work at 6 am in the morning. He would leave around 2 am (no sex y'all)! Every Friday, when he got off, he would come to see me and I would leave on Sunday around 2 am. He would get a hotel room for himself. I had my own place, but he was very respectful! He would take me out on dates and go to church with me. He was a bit older than I was. I had a conversation with God. I said, "God, is this the man You want me to have?" He said, "Yes." Well, I didn't ask no mo.

Time went by and we ended up having sex. We tried to wait. God beat me up so bad! I went to him and said, "Hey, we can't do that no more unless we married." And I wasn't playing! The conviction was real! So in my mind, this wasn't going to last much longer because all the jokers I had been with left me if they weren't getting "it." They were out! But he said, "Lisa, I told you. I'm not going anywhere!" So he still came as usual. And we ended up getting married!

A few months later, I had to make some decisions. It was hard to leave my church and my family. I started to look for a church in Baltimore because I knew I couldn't lay down and let the devil play on me. I had to stay grounded in the Word. I moved to Baltimore and attended church the first week I moved and I am still there today in 2021. Thank you, Jesus.

The love from the door drew me right in. Me being married for the first time, I wanted to give my husband a child. But I still hadn't forgiven myself and thought God was mad at me for having an abortion. So I prayed harder, fasting and praying for forgiveness. I was believing for a baby and God was elevating my faith. God started to deliver me from the weed and through the teachings, I learned a lot and I found out you have to get with someone who has passed the test you're in.

I opened up to a lady at church and I didn't want to because I had been judged all my life. But she said, "I will pray with you." I asked my husband to pray also. My pastor prayed for us as well.

During a fast that I was on, God spoke. God said, "Go upstairs and drink the oil." I did that and have not had a black and mild or weed for three years. I got baptized. My husband joined the church the same day. God was answering my prayers. He heard my heart. One Sunday, I saw my husband kneeling on the altar. God spoke to me and said, "Your house is never going to be the same." Little did I know, the next month, we were pregnant. Look at God! At 39 years old, I was pregnant, y'all. She was born on Dec 19, a healthy, beautiful baby girl, Madison. She's our miracle baby.

God was with me in the valley and He's with you too. Don't give up on God because He won't give up on you. Eyes haven't seen and ears haven't heard. If He did it for me, He will do it for you. Give it all to God! Be patient! Have respect and pray. Don't try Him. Trust Him! The only thing I can say is, "But God!"

I never thought I would be in this place in my life and God is not through with me yet, just like

He is not through with you as you are reading this right now! Just ask God to lead and give your life over to Him. Leave everything in His hands. He is the Potter. Ask Him to lead you to the place of worship where He wants you to be.

You don't have to do this alone. He is waiting to hear from you. Nothing is hard for God. He will forgive you, but you have to ask! It is time to forgive yourself and forgive others. Remember Jesus loves you just the way you are, but too much to let you stay that way.

Thank you, Lord, for choosing me, loving me, forgiving me and cleaning me up.

I remember before moving, I was riding with a Minister from my former church and she said to me, "When you get to Baltimore, you can write the book!" I said, "Who? Me?" So here I am…I'm living proof that God is a good Father. I'm living proof that when you get out of your way, put God first, repent, pray, and turn from your wicked ways, everything will shift. It may not be peaches and cream, but God will provide in many ways.

My Encouraging Words to You...

Dear men and ladies, young, middle-aged and old…

Never give up on God because He won't give up on you. As I look back over my life, He was with me in my darkest places, when I couldn't defend myself, when I was motherless and fatherless and when I didn't love myself.

If He can save me, He can do the same for you. Seek His face while He still can be found. Trust the process. Have faith. It's not easy and sometimes, it gets really rough, but God will see you through. If nobody else loves you, know that God always loves you.

Woman, man… You're worth it.

Even when you don't see God working, He's working! Don't let people deceive you and say everything's going to be okay, when you get saved. Truth be told, the fire is turned up because, for one, the devil doesn't want to let you go. Keep going through. There is a process before the promise! Forgive yourself, repent and don't go back to your wicked ways. You can't take everyone with you. Everyone's not going to cheer you on, but love them anyway. Be sure to listen to what God says. He will order your steps.

I want to tell you that today, my mother and I are in a great space and she is a wonderful nana to all her grands. My real father and I are cool. My dad is still amazing and doesn't look at me any different.

I thank God for every single thing I have been through. It has made me stronger and wiser. It has taught me to value and forgive people. God has truly taught me how to love again.

He is teaching me how to be a servant, wife, and mother. He wants me to be more and more like Him each day. I pray you let God mold you and teach you! Talk to God and genuinely pray. Find a Bible-based church filled with the Holy Spirit and love. Ask God to order your steps, change you and renew your mind.

I was a drunk, drug addict, thief, fighter and more, but I know that God is able. God's not done with me. Only God helped me because where I'm from, people judge you before asking you why you're doing something or go by what someone else told them about you instead of getting to know you for themselves.

Even when I started going to church, these folks said to my former Pastor, "Lisa? Does she go to your church? Do you know her and what she has done?" Thank goodness she was a true woman of God. My former Pastor had a saying…. "God loves you just the way you are but too much to let you stay that way... Always remember that."

And my now Bishop's saying is…. "God is never late or early. He's right on time… Trust the process. It's hard, but it's fair…." So please, do not let people or the enemy through people to get you off course.

There were times, I just didn't want to live anymore. I was tired of being rejected, lost and unloved. I didn't love myself or care how I looked or anything. At times, I didn't even have clothes to put on and was wearing a friend's clothes. It was rough, but God. There were days I went without food, even when I had a job and living on my own.

Today, I'm in a better place. I am closer to God, loving myself, being a wife, and stay-at-home. Sometimes, I can't believe it myself, but God saw this day. I thought God hated me for having an abortion. After the abortion, I had many mental breakdowns. It seemed like I could hear a baby saying, "Mommy, it's not your fault."

I just recently forgave myself, but also gave guilt offerings before I truly understood God's forgiveness. God did not require me to give guilt offerings. I took that upon myself, because I didn't think that I would ever be free from that.

All my life, until I met my now husband, men have used and abused me. Besides my uncle, my mom's brother, always had my back, thick and thin, right or wrong.

There were times I didn't like my mom or dad. But recently, God dealt with me, and I had to stop judging them, forgave them and moved on. But maybe my mother was just like me was hiding, holding things in and running from the pain. Some things we will never know because that's how our culture is set up sadly. But I decree and declare the generational curses stop with me!! As I look back, God didn't only save me on that operating table. He began to change me! I remember waking up in the recovery room with a chest tube. I was about that tough, gangster life. Hell, the whole eastern shore was calling me O.G., but I was tired of fighting and definitely tired of proving a point to people.

Now I see God uses what you use to do in the Kingdom in a good way. Now, I know how to fight and go to war in prayer. Won't He do it?

So many times, I know it could've and should've been dead…but God!! He loved me, when I didn't love myself. He kept me, when I didn't want to be kept. He saved a sinner like me.

I can say today that I love me some me! I'm not perfect by a long shot, but I'm no way near who I used to be. As the songwriter says, "I thank you for it all."

I thank God for my husband. He makes it so easy to love him. He prays with and for me. There are no secrets, no lock codes, and no wondering if he's out with other women. He dates only me and constantly reminds me how much he loves me. The song by Tamia, "Still," is really real like us. Are we perfect? No, but we are perfect for each other! He loves some Lisa and I love me some him. He supports me, provides!!! He's patient, kind.

I'm living proof of what God can and will do. Don't worry about what people say or think. Just keep looking to the hills. That's where your help comes from. Let God change your identity.

He did it for me. From 9th Grade until even now, people still call me O.G. Some didn't even know my name is Lisa. Sometimes, when people call me O.G. now, I'm quick to say, "No, she's dead. It's Lisa." I remember when I first got saved. I prayed and asked God to remove anyone and anything not pleasing in His sight. I was down to one or two real people or friends. God removed almost everyone. I was wowed. I felt like, "So none of them were really my freaking friends." But now I know, see, and understand what God was showing me. If I was an O.G. for the devil, I sure can be one for God. He knows my name. People will now see the God in me.

Sidenote: *Pray, Pray, Pray! Prayer is the key to your total breakthrough.*

Over the years, I held back so many tears. Now, I've been crying a river. It's okay to cry. People expected me to be strong and tough, so I put it on like I did clothes. But now, God is my strength and my refuge!

So now, at 40, I'm going back to school for my GED and I feel darn good about it. All I can say is this is just the beginning. I can't wait to see what God continues to unfold in my life.

The best is yet to come!

About The Author

Lisa Duffy-Finney, is a prime example of what God will do. She has overcome child molestation, drug addiction and alcohol abuse. Lisa is now living for the Lord whole heartedly, with her husband and one year old daughter. Lisa's mission is to spread God's word as a witness.

Made in the USA
Columbia, SC
10 August 2024

39765622R00030